THE MASK OF DRUG ADDICTION

HOW IT CAN MAKE OR BREAK A FAMILY

KEASHA HAYTHE

Published by Victorious You Press™

While the author has made every effort to ensure that the ideas, statistics, and information presented in this Book are accurate to the best of his/her abilities, any implications direct, derived, or perceived, should only be used at the reader's discretion. The author cannot be held responsible for any personal or commercial damage arising from communication, application, or misinterpretation of the information presented herein.

Printed in the United States of America

ISBN: 978-1-952756-43-6

For details email vyp.joantrandall@gmail.com
or visit us at www.victoriousyoupress.com

TABLE OF CONTENTS

FOREWORD

Have you ever said to yourself, "This is just too much, I can't do this anymore? How much can one person take?" As a married woman, have you ever thought, "What have I gotten myself into?" If you answered yes, this book is definitely for you. It is my privilege to help Keasha deliver her story of overcoming, perseverance, and trusting God through the most challenging times. Often during tough times, we allow our emotions to control how we handle things instead of drawing closer to God to guide us through hard times with a peace of mind and wisdom.

I have counseled and encouraged thousands of women who have reached the point of giving up. I am continually reminding them where they are currently in their relationship and life does not have to be their last chapter and through the strength and power they have in Jesus, life can be sweet no matter the situation.

We are much stronger than we often give ourselves credit. Keasha so openly shares the steps she took to turn her family's tragedy into triumph. By the time you finish this book, it will empower you to do the same.

Dr. DeeDee Freeman

Spirit of Faith Christian Center

Chapter I
The Fantasy

Late one night my one-year-old daughter and I were in bed asleep and woke up to the smoke detector going off. We got up and walked to the kitchen to find a grease fire raging on the stove. Our screaming woke up my 10-year-old son and my husband and when my husband rushed to put out the fire, grease splashed on him, catching his hand and arm on fire. As we stood there watching him burn right before our eyes, it felt as if we were in a scene from a Hollywood movie.

As a young girl, I had a vision of a white picket fence, a two-story house on plenty of land with a long driveway leading to the house. Also in the vision was a highly sought after VP position in a prominent Fortune 500 company, a six-figure salary with money in the bank and a fully loaded red BMW in the garage. Like most young girls, I dreamed about my future and what I wanted it to look like. I wanted to be married to a man who was a good husband, whatever that meant, but I wanted him to be a smart man with a plan who knew what he wanted out of life and how he was going to get there! While growing up my examples were my aunts and the parents of my friends. My mother was not married and neither of my grandmothers were ever married, but what I learned from all of my examples was husbands were to protect and provide for their wives and family.

As a teenager, I met the love of my life and prayed to God one day he would be my husband. There was something about John. I knew he was the one from the first time we met because something on the inside told me he was the one. We would talk for hours. He understood the importance of having a career path and being a good provider and I thought maybe, just maybe, God heard my prayers. John had a promising future, a good-paying job, and was saving money while going to technical school to be a mechanic. We started seeing each other, and I became pregnant with our first daughter.

I remember, vividly, the time I was having severe cramps and didn't know what it was. I kept all of my prenatal appointments, but I didn't pay attention. I was not aware of the signs of a miscarriage, and I twisted and turned all night in pain. When I got up in the morning to go to the bathroom, little did I know I was in labor. By the time I arrived at the hospital that morning, I could barely walk and had to be rushed to the maternity ward and delivered our daughter within minutes. She lived for 20 minutes.

John and my mother were with me at the hospital and when John saw the baby was not breathing, he became weak in his knees and could barely stand. In that moment I saw his compassion and how hurt he was to lose a child and it was a devastating time for each of us.

As young as John and I were, we had to make burial arrangements for our daughter, who we named Kierra Marchelle. Thankful for the support of my mother, who made and decorated a small casket for Kierra, we purchased a burial plot, held a burial at the cemetery and experienced something I never wanted to experience again.

John and I continued to see each other, off and on, and in my senior year of high school, I was pregnant again. This time, I carried our child to full term. I graduated from high school at 17 and began planning our future together. Four months after graduation and one week before my 18th birthday, I gave birth. Being a teenage mother was not part of my vision for the future but I was careless in protecting myself. I felt horrible about becoming pregnant, and this meant my plans of going to college were definitely on hold. I was feeling sorry for myself and asking how in the world did I get caught up and be so stupid to do something like this again? My parents were teenage parents and my father always talked to me about sex and pregnancy, and here I was doing the same thing — continuing a generational cycle. I knew better, but I sure wasn't acting like it.

In my heart of hearts, I knew it was wrong and so many people were disappointed when I became pregnant a second time but I made a promise to myself I would take college courses at the local community college and not have another child until I was married. I realized I was trying to fill a void and was looking for love in all the wrong places. Love would not come from sex or anything else, and what I realized was, I did not love myself. I also realized I had to fill that internal void and learn to love myself before I could love others.

Early in my life I accepted so much disrespect in my relationships because, just like many women, I thought I could change the things I didn't like in my boyfriend before or after he became my husband. After the birth of our son John Jr., I knew the marriage proposal would come soon. Well, let me tell you, one year turned into two, then three, then four, all the way up to ten. Ten years of waiting for the marriage dream to come true. If only I had realized my worth. I am definitely in a much different place today because I would never wait 10 years for a man to propose to me, which is a revelation that comes from wisdom and age.

Well, time passed and it was the most wonderful time of the year. Christmas was coming! We were feeling excited and had a beautiful tree with lots of gifts under it for our son. We were all filled with happiness and John asked me to open my gift. He had purchased a one carat round diamond engagement ring as my Christmas gift, placed it on my finger that Christmas morning and asked me to marry him. I called my mother, my grandmother and my aunties to tell them the good news. Finally, I can begin planning that little girl's dream–I can now plan my wedding. It took us about a year to plan and save for the wedding, and during this time, I quit my full-time banking job and was working part time in an accounting office. John and I attended a series of marital counseling appointments with the pastor who would perform our ceremony. We went through months of counseling and during our counseling sessions we took a test to see where our greatest challenges would be. The results concluded our greatest marital challenge would be in our finances. We brushed it off as something we would just keep our eyes on.

After we completed the counseling, our families helped us plan our special day. It was a beautiful day in May, and our family and friends had gathered near the water to support us. I wore a gorgeous white fitted sequined off the shoulder wedding gown and our bridesmaids were dressed in beautiful burgundy dresses with a satin neckline and a chiffon scarf. My husband was in his black tuxedo with a burgundy vest, my son had on his black tuxedo, and the groomsmen were all looking dapper. We gathered at the church and were ready. I took in a deep breath and as the music played, I had tears of joy in my eyes as my step-father walked me down the aisle, encouraging me every step of the way. We said our vows, exchanged rings and kissed. We are now in a covenant relationship in the sight of God until death do us part. After greeting our guests at the entrance door, we were ready to release white doves as a symbol of love, peace, and the Holy Spirit. John held one dove, I held one, and our son held another one, and on the count of three, we released them into the air. We released the nine remaining doves, they circled above once, and away they flew. We had a wonderful time of taking pictures, attended the wedding reception, sang, danced and had so much fun with family and friends. It was a day we would both cherish and remember forever. I was happy and so ready to start our life together. The honeymoon was great. This union was meant to be and this marriage will last forever; no storms — just perfection.

Well, the first year went by and life was grand. We had our second child, a beautiful baby girl named Makayla Nicole, exactly what John and I both wanted. As we were learning to become one and operate as husband and wife, my career had just begun and things were falling into place.

Almost two years into our marriage, John started acting differently and I couldn't figure out what was happening. We would argue, he would go out with the fellas and I would retaliate by going out with the girls. I felt uncomfortable going out because clubs were not my thing and I just didn't feel right being there. I felt there had to be more to doing life than what I was experiencing, and there was still such a void needing to be filled. Getting married did not fill the void I had inside, so I knew I had to do something different.

I thought attending church would be a good place to help me make sense of what was going on in my marriage and I remembered a non-denominational church my stepfather had taken us to a while back. Let me start by saying I never "belonged" to a church. In fact, when I was about 10 years old, I went to a local church with my aunt and uncle after my cousin died in a car accident. During the service, the pastor called all the kids up for prayer. I didn't go up with the other kids, when the pastor asked me after the service if I had come up with the other kids I lied and told him, yes. He must have prayed a special prayer for me knowing I had lied to him in church, but back then I didn't know any better and didn't think it mattered. I had already seen a lot at such a young age and I remember telling my cousin I didn't believe in God, which shocked her to hear me say that, but it was true. How did I know God was real?

Early one Sunday morning I got up and told my husband I was going to church and when I walked up the steps to the sanctuary, I felt love and peace, which is the best way I can describe what I felt. As I listened to the preacher, I knew I was in the exact place I needed to be.

For months I attended that church and when John attended we began attending as a family. One Sunday, the pastor had an altar call for anyone wanting to be saved. We all went to the altar to receive salvation and accepted Jesus Christ as our Lord and Savior, and shortly after that, we were both baptized. When I was growing up, I never heard about any of this so I was not familiar with salvation, being born again or being baptized. I thought, "I will give this saved life a try. What do I have to lose? Either God is real or he isn't."

Things were looking good, and now that we were saved, nothing would go wrong because we were on God's side. Well, no one told me what to expect after getting saved so I was in la-la land walking around on Cloud 9 thinking nothing bad was going to happen in my life now that we were "saved", but I still had questions, like what does "saved" mean?

Knowing I needed to know more about this relationship with Jesus we just started, I started attending bible study to learn all I could about the bible and the teachings of Jesus Christ. I took it one day at a time and read as much as I could every day. One evening as I was leaving bible study, my cousin, who was also a member, asked how my husband was doing. "He's doing good," I said. Then she asked, "Do you know why he keeps nodding off?" With a perplexed look on my face, I said, "Huh??" "Heroin makes you nod off," she continued. I stood there with a confused look on my face and she repeated her statement. "Heroin makes you nod off", then she walked away.

I just stood there stunned and after regaining my composure I walked over to the co-pastor of our church and repeated to her the conversation I just had with my cousin. "Why would she say that to you? How would she know?" she asked. Then I remembered my cousin used to be a drug user. I broke down crying as my co-pastor comforted me, prayed for me, and then told me to go home and talk to my husband. I had to find out what my cousin was talking about, but I knew at that point I was not alone.

There was someone praying and standing with me through this ordeal.

Chapter II
The Pain

This was not the marriage I signed up for! What was happening to my life? John was in a lot of pain as the emergency room staff tried to ease the pain which resulted from him burning his arm and hand. I could hear the agony in his voice as the nurses were telling him to hold his hand down in a bowl of cool water to make it feel better. Despite the morphine and other pain medication, John's pain did not stop. After hours in the emergency room, the doctors determined the severity of his burns warranted him being treated at a burn center two hours away. It was 1:00 a.m. and while he was being transported by ambulance to the burn center, the EMT knew exactly what to do to stop the pain. He told John to hold his arm up and immediately his arm stopped throbbing. Something so simple seemed so easy, right? Why couldn't the doctors or nurses at the hospital have told him to do that? They should have noticed the severity of his burns as soon as he went busting through the emergency room doors. That local hospital was just not equipped to treat him.

After being admitted into the burn center, John's blood pressure rose to deadly levels. The nurses tried everything they knew to get his blood pressure down and nothing was working. One of the attending nurses sat with me in the waiting room and asked me a lot of questions. I answered what I could and told her he was taking blood pressure medication, and that was all I was aware of. Right then is when the conversation with my cousin came back to my mind and I wondered if what John was experiencing was drug-related. I went to John's room where the nurse was still attending to him and asked her to step outside of the room for a one-on-one conversation. She made a note when I told her I suspected drugs and she returned to the room to have a conversation with John. I watched from the hallway outside the room as she spoke with John, and all I could see were tears streaming down his face. The nurse came out of the room and told me she would administer a drug to lower his blood pressure, which was elevated because he was going through withdrawal. I'm sure after she explained to John he was facing a life or death situation and his proper treatment would depend on his honesty, he finally admitted he had used drugs days before. When the nurse told me he was going through withdrawal, everything came into perspective. I felt numb, as if I had been hoodwinked, bamboozled, and sucker-punched. I walked into the room and saw guilt and shame all over his face. He cried and could hardly look at me, and even though I was angry, I knew it was not the time to have a conversation about his drug use. It would have been a heated conversation, and the hospital was not the place to have it.

I was in a state of bewilderment after John's admission of being hooked on snorting heroin. What was I going to do? How could I have not known? How could he do this to me and his family? I'm saved and trying to do right. Why me, Lord? Why? And God answered; "Why not you? My son was beaten, bruised, and nailed to the cross for you, so why not you?" This is a light affliction.

Chapter III
The Promise

Traveling to and from the hospital over the next few weeks to see John took an emotional toll on the family and I was furious. One day as I walked through the burn center, I could smell the flesh of so many other burn victims. Not only were there adults, but there were also children who had suffered burns all over their bodies. When I looked around me and saw how many people were there, I thanked God, realizing our situation could have been much worse. I was thankful for God's protection, realizing my entire family could have suffered burns in the fire.

John's burns were so bad they thought skin graphs on his hand would be necessary. In order to be discharged, John had to be able to move his fingers, so the nurses worked with him day and night. I knew the Lord was faithful to all His promises and loving toward all He has made, so as we prayed, I told John to trust God and he would be able to move his fingers soon. I was still trying to figure out what God meant by "why not me" when I was suddenly reminded of John 3:16 (KJV): For God so loved the world, that he gave his only begotten Son that whosoever believeth in him, should not perish, but have everlasting life.

God meant Jesus Christ suffered for my sins and God loved me so much He gave His only son. What pain could be worse than Jesus being beaten, spit on, hung on the cross and pierced in his body? The hurt and pain I was experiencing was nowhere near the pain Jesus felt as he suffered and died on the cross for all humanity.

God revealed many things to me regarding our future, our purpose and destiny, and even showed us working together in ministry. He showed me our future home and some other things in store for us. Psalm 145:13 (NIV) Your kingdom is an everlasting kingdom, and your dominion endures through all generations. The Lord is trustworthy in all he promises and faithful in all he does. This was one scripture I meditated on daily. In order for me to stand and believe my husband was going to overcome his drug addiction and be free, I had to trust God — I mean really trust God. I had to have an honest talk with God and say to him, "God, either you are real or you are not. If you are real and if the bible is true, this situation was going to work out." It was time for me to put my big girl panties on and buckle up for the roller coaster ride.

Lord knows, I was a babe in Christ, but I had to know if this Christian life was real.

When John could finally return home from the hospital, we had a conversation about how he was planning to beat his drug addiction. Initially, he didn't want to talk about it, but when he shared a little about how he started using drugs, he ended the conversation with "I can stop whenever I want." "Sure you can," I thought. "Isn't that what everyone says?"

John did things his way and even though I thought it was way too soon, he went back to work part-time and injured his hand even more. He was a collision repair technician and for the past 10 years, that was his life. He loved what he did and he was good at it, but we didn't know if he could ever repair cars again. We immediately lost his income; because of his injuries, he could not work. We had two children to feed, one in daycare, and a huge car payment. I wondered how in the world I was going to maintain a household on my salary of $20,000.00 per year. I did what I was being taught to do, which was stand on the word of God. I wrote down scriptures and God gave me Proverbs 3:5 (NIV) Trust in the LORD with all your heart and lean not on your own understanding; in all your ways submit to him, and he will make your paths straight.

The vision the Lord showed me meant my husband would be delivered and set free from drug addiction, so I had to act like my husband was already free and see him that way. No matter what my reality was, and even though I didn't see it at the moment, I had to operate by faith and believe what God had shown me.

My sister had given me, as a gift, a book by Stormie O'Martin entitled The Power of a Praying Wife. I began reading that book, and little did I know it would be exactly what I needed. As I read through the book, I began praying the prayers and studying the bible more every day. I attended church and started taking ministerial classes, but it seemed the more I studied and prayed, the rougher my life became. Day in and day out, I saw no change and even though I kept going, I still saw no change. Things were not getting better and I wanted to give up and leave. It was as if my husband did not care about himself or his family. Drugs came first and the relapses came too often. He would stop, use again, stop and use again. We were all living in his mother's house, but things got so bad I wanted to take our two children and leave. I tried to get an apartment, but my credit wasn't good enough and there was a waiting list for the government housing programs. I didn't want to move to where my mother was because she was in another state and my grandmother, who was my rock, had passed away. I had little money in the bank, two kids, and no home of my own. I felt defeated and helpless and knew I had to fight my way out of that valley experience.

My children and I eventually left to stay with a family member, and even though she made us feel welcome, I still felt we were a burden. She had her daily routine as a single woman with two dogs, and I felt we were encroaching on her space. God showed me the scripture 1 Corinthians 7:13 (NIV) And if a woman has a husband who is not a believer and he is willing to live with her, she must not divorce him. After two weeks we returned to

John's mother's home and I continued to stand on the promises of God.

Chapter IV
The Reality vs The Truth

As time passed, one step forward yielded ten steps backward. We were four years into our marriage and I felt like I was living in hell on earth. Although I didn't share my situation with many, I knew there were a few people at church who were truly interceding for my family. We were in intercessory prayer every Wednesday night praying, not only for my family, but for others as well.

As a family of four living on my salary, we were living at poverty level; and let's not even talk about debt because my credit was jacked up. According to the U.S. Census Bureau, 11.8% of the U.S. population is living in poverty—earning below $25,750. Since my husband was not working, I had to get myself together to do things I had never done before and I didn't know where to start. I went to Social Services to get some kind of help for my family.

Let me tell you, I was already feeling down and humiliated because I was in this predicament, but the employees of these governmental agencies were horrible. They acted as if they had never fallen on hard times or it was my fault I needed help. I had mouths to feed and had to do what I had to do. They had no compassion and showed no kindness or sense of urgency to assist. Now, I know some people try to work the system, but for those who honestly need help, help them! Don't make them jump through a bunch of hoops to get help. I felt like I gave them so much information the next step would be them needing to take my blood. Everyone in the social services office seemed to be miserable, and I would treat no one the way I was treated. I was being humbled through such a humiliating process. Eventually I was assigned to a service worker who was kind and seemed willing to help. I ended up with approximately $100 in food stamps to feed a family of four and one-time help to assist with childcare. Childcare was $120 per week, so government assistance is overrated and not the answer for me. I re-enrolled part-time at a local community college to get a degree because I knew I had to keep grinding and increase my education in order to not only get us out, but to make sure we did not continue to live a life of poverty.

The hole was getting deeper and I felt like I was sinking in quicksand. I could not pay our bills and needed food stamps to feed the family. Bill collectors were calling to collect on past due bills and asking stupid questions like "Can you make a payment today over the phone?" "No fool, what don't you understand? We have no money to pay you."

At one point, everyone in the house was screening phone calls and if the call was an "out of area" number, we didn't answer because we knew it was a bill collector. I was determined this would not be our life, so I began giving. I gave my time at church and on the little salary I had, I gave tithes and offerings. In fact, I increased my tithing and trusted God more and more. I also researched tithing and allowed my heart and not my mind to lead me. When my family was saying "you better not be giving all your money to that church," I became a cheerful giver and followed the word precept upon precept, still tithing and giving cheerfully from my heart. I said, "God, if you are true and your word is real, I am holding you at your word and I believe you are going to bring us out of this dark pit we are in. You say in your word you will never leave me nor forsake me and you shall supply all of my needs according to your riches in Glory. God, I need you to supply all of my needs, right now". When I started giving, blessings started flowing and God sent people our way with food, checks came in the mail, and I was in awe of the support, love and acts of kindness. The only thing I was doing was praying and, without me saying a word, friends from the church would drop by with things we needed.

The drug addiction was like a see-saw, and during it all the children were being affected. One evening John used the car and went out with friends. I was home with the children and when I put them to bed for the night, I was tired and also went to bed as well. When I woke up, it was 2:00 a.m. and I noticed John was not home. I worried something may have happened to him and must have dialed his cell phone number over 50 times, leaving a message each time before finally calling the police. I gave them all the information they needed about the car and after a couple of hours had passed, they called to let me know the car had been located in the city. I knew John had a friend in the city, and I also knew he was no good. Antonio was always in trouble and couldn't stay out of jail to save his life.

When John came home that morning he had nothing but excuses but it was obvious he had been out getting high with Antonio and their other "get high together" buddies. As soon as I knew who those other buddies were, I kept them out of the house and away from us. After that, John made a decision to get help and went to rehab. Things improved and he seemed to be trying to kick the habit and get clean, not only for himself but for his family. After getting out of rehab, John received a call from his aunt in Virginia asking him to go with her to pick up his sick father who was in Brooklyn, New York. He agreed to go with her and when they got to New York, John was in shock. When John was young, his father walked out of the house to get cigarettes and never came back to his wife or child. Now as a 36-year-old man, John is seeing his father again and those emotions which had been suppressed since he was a little boy were coming back. Little did I know, that little boy was still in there and had never found peace or closure. To me, this was the unhealed hurt manifesting in the form of drug use and mental and physical abuse. This little boy had never healed from the emotional toll of his father walking away and this little boy had never healed from not having a father or proper upbringing to teach him how to be a loving man, father, and husband.

The U.S. Census reports 38.7 percent of African-American minors live with both parents and a disproportionate number of black children under 18 live in single-parent households. The Brookings Institute wrote an article stating out-of-wedlock birth rates have soared since 1970. In 1965, 24% of black infants and 3.1% of white infants were born to single mothers. By 1990 the rates had risen to 64% for black infants and 18% for whites. Every year, about one million more children are born into fatherless families. If we have learned any policy lesson well over the past 25 years, it is that for children living in single-parent homes, the odds of living in poverty are great.

These statistics shed a light on why there are broken relationships and a lack of emotional healing in families. Cycles of abuse take an emotional toll on a child and in order to stop the cycle, it is important for even children to get the help they need. We need to be comfortable seeing a therapist and feeling it is okay so the cycle does not continue. Most times, therapy is needed at an early age, but the need may go unfulfilled or unnoticed by the parent. Perhaps the parent does not believe in therapy or they may not realize how certain things affect a young child, but unless a child receives positive treatment to effectively identify issues and troubling behavior, the problems will persist.

Getting back to my husband — when he saw his father, he was not prepared for what he saw. His father looked nothing like he remembered him as a child. His aunt waited until they got to New York to tell him his father had cancer. After picking up his father and before getting him back to Virginia, we prayed and his father received Christ. While walking into church for service the next day, we received a call his father had passed away that morning.

As we traveled to Virginia for the funeral, I realized the death of John's father could trigger him and potentially set him back. I wanted to be as supportive and sensitive to his emotions as I could. I noticed he was keeping things inside and although he would talk a little, he would not fully communicate his feelings. After returning home from the funeral services, I took a pregnancy test and found out I was pregnant with our third child. I cried yet again — the plan was two children. God, you must think this is funny. I know what you may be thinking; why would she get pregnant in the midst of all she is going through? Yep, I said the same thing, except to God. We were using protection, but guess what? It failed us!!

I was not ready to bring another child into this world of dysfunction, but the baby was coming. I thought to myself, "isn't there a saying - when death comes sometimes a new birth comes?" When I told John about the pregnancy, he was happy about it. We discussed baby names and talked about whether we thought it would be a boy or a girl. Months went by and things were going well, like old times. I received a promotion at work so my salary was increasing, our doctor appointments were normal and the baby was growing.

About six months into the pregnancy, I began having mild contractions and the doctor advised me to go on bed rest until at least 37 ½ weeks. This meant I had to stop working and take leave. I wanted to make sure I kept my stress level down since I had two previous miscarriages. I am not sure how we got through, but we did.

When we decided we wanted to find out the sex of the baby, the doctor showed us it was a boy. At that moment, we knew we would name him after John's father. I wanted a biblical name, so we decided on David William. In the bible, David was a king and I knew there was a calling on the life of this baby boy. We used a Mickey Mouse theme, painted, added a border and continued to get the room ready. I was on bed rest for the rest of the pregnancy and finally, early one Sunday morning, I began having contractions. I called my mother and mother-in-law and they met us at the hospital. I had my gospel music ready to play during delivery. This was my third time, and the third time is a charm. When we get to the hospital, they check me in, get me settled into a room and begin hooking me up to monitors and asking if I wanted an epidural.

"No thank you, I have delivered all of our children without one, so I'll pass on you sticking that long needle in my back."

The contractions were coming, it was time for the doctor to come in help me push this baby boy out and as I am breathing and breathing, the doctor says, "PUSH!" He paused and said, "Wait a minute, the baby is upside down and I have to turn him around," at which point he reaches in and turns the baby around. Several more pushes and here the baby comes crying out of the womb. What an incredible moment. Our baby boy was here and I had tears of joy.

Along with the tears of joy came a bunch of what looked like grapes protruding from my butt. The nurses were in shock and didn't know exactly what to say to me, so they began discussing a previous delivery of a woman who had a problem with hemorrhoids, except her hemorrhoids were the size of a raisin. One nurse mentioned she had never seen hemorrhoids the size of the ones I had, and the next day the doctor sliced them to remove the clots. Talk about painful! That pain was worse than giving birth!

I was in the hospital for two days and with the recent change in our lives, John seemed to have been recovering and getting back to normal one day at a time. After returning home from the hospital, I went into the bedroom and saw a bottle of pink liquid on the floor beside our bed. I picked it up, asked John what it was, and he told me it was methadone. I said, "what in the hell is methadone doing on the bedroom floor where Makayla could reach it?" He didn't respond and my heart dropped to the floor because I knew what methadone was and what it was used for.

The mere thought of me being in the hospital after giving birth to our son and John being home with our four-year-old daughter self-dosing with methadone made me so mad I could have killed him. Our daughter could have picked up the bottle, opened it, drank its contents, and died. John was out of control and irresponsible, and I knew he could not be trusted to be home alone with our children. From that point forward, I planned for someone to stay with the children whenever I was going to be away. I cried and cried, thanking God for His protection which surrounded our children, but I also knew this matter had to be resolved. John and I had a long talk and I told him he had to get help to get clean. He was in complete denial and claimed he was in control and could quit at any time.

I needed help and didn't know where to turn. For the first time in my life, I was being humbled and had sincere empathy for those addicted to drugs. I started researching to find out how I could help my husband and what signs I needed to look for.

Since the 1970s, we have been waging a war on drugs. Vox reported the U.S. spent $1 trillion on the drug war and made 45 million drug arrests. The vast majority of drug law violation arrests are for possession (84 percent). Much of the problem can be attributed to an inadequate public health system lacking the capacity and funding for effective substance abuse treatment.

According to Psychology Today, there are over 22 million individuals in the U.S. who have a substance abuse problem (including alcohol). There are about 4.5 million individuals who have a substance use disorder because of the abuse of illicit and prescription drugs. The public health consequences of substance abuse are staggering. There were over 70,000 drug overdose deaths in 2017, the majority attributed to opioids, which represents a doubling of drug-related deaths in just 10 years.

CDC Stats:

- In 2017, there were 70,237 drug overdose deaths in the United States.
- The rates of drug overdose deaths increased from 1999 to 2017 for all age groups studied.
- The rate of drug overdose deaths involving heroin increased from 0.7 in 1999 to 1.0 in 2008 to 4.9 in 2016. The rate in 2017 and 2016 were the same.

John and I started working together on his addiction and, as anyone could imagine, moods were up and down; one day good and the next day it was bad. Living with an addict was a daily struggle, and he used his addiction as an excuse not to work. It had been years since he had a job and he was not looking for one. I wasn't going to feed a grown man, so I stopped cooking. I know it may sound harsh but, in my mind, I thought tough love would make him want to get a job so he would be able to eat. Instead of cooking meals, I took the kids to places with cheap kids' meals, leaving him to find his food and cook for himself. I developed an attitude of "if you are willing and able to work, it's time to get a job. It doesn't matter what the job is — get one" and I took the bible verse in 2 Thessalonians Chapter 3:10 (NIV) seriously "If a man will not work, he shall not eat."

I didn't understand how drugs affected the brain and as the withdrawal symptoms came and left, John suffered alone in pain. He was weak, stayed in the bed all day with the curtains closed and the room dark and even though we were still going to church, praying, and doing all we were taught to do to be free, it looked like he was slipping into depression.

Although my husband may have had a desire to serve God, because of his condition, the addiction was winning. I would ask him if he had prayed, and his response would be "yes". I thought him praying was a good start and when asked if he had prayed for me and our family, his response was "no, just my normal prayer." His "normal" prayer was "cover me during the day and lead me." I asked him, "When are you going to graduate from your kindergarten prayer?" In all seriousness, when you are serving God and He is the head of your life, as the wife, you want a husband who covers you in prayer, otherwise how are the two of you going to walk together in agreement?

Chapter V
The Mask Revealed

Our son took ill and had to be hospitalized, which meant my husband had to be home with the other two children. A family member was there to monitor the house. At first, I was fearful, but then a sense of peace came over me. While our son was in the hospital, John came by once and stayed for a few hours while I went home to shower and get more clothes. Late one night, I received a call from John and he sounded as if he was hallucinating. I was on the phone with him for about an hour as he told me people were after him and were outside watching the house. So, here I am at the hospital with our 3-year-old son and John is at home with our 7-year-old daughter and our 15-year-old son. The only thing I could do was pray and reach out to my friend, Ann, to pray with me. I would not let the enemy put fear in me. God had protected us this far, and I knew he would protect us this time too. Eventually the conversation ended because John was so tired he had to go to bed. That was one of those nights I felt like I had no control. I could not protect my kids and I felt helpless. My emotions were running wild, wondering when this nightmare was going to be over. We had been in this nightmare for eight years and I wanted out. I started wondering when I was going to experience a real marriage with a husband who loved the Lord, himself, and his family more than he loved drugs.

When I finally got off the phone with John, I called John Jr. and I told him to watch out for anything strange happening inside or outside the house and to call me right away if he saw anything out of the ordinary. One day later, our son was released from the hospital and we could go home. I looked for a place to live and came up empty. I applied for Section-8 housing, letting them know I was in an abusive living environment, but still nothing. I could not get out of this living situation — I had no place to go.

My mother-in-law was a nurse with experience working in an addiction facility, but when I tried to talk to her about her son, she denied the fact he was even on drugs. I turned to my church family. If you find yourself in a similar situation, pray this prayer — this is the prayer I prayed:

Father, In the Name of Jesus, I acknowledge you as Lord of my life, I submit to thy will and not my will. Lord, I trust in you to lead, guide, and direct my path. (Proverbs 3:5-6)

For we know, that all things work together for good to those that love God and who are called according to His purpose (Romans 8:28). Lord I give this burden to you, for your yoke is easy and your burden is light. (Matthew 11:30)

Thank you, Lord, for hearing me and delivering my husband from his addiction. I decree and declare I am victorious in this situation and the enemy is under my feet. In Jesus' name, Amen.

When John and I would go to church services, he would nod off in church and I remember the night when he came into bible study late and high. I could not even look at him. We closed our bible study in prayer and as everyone left there were about five of us still in the church. Our co-pastor said, "let's pray for John." As they prayed for him, and he fell down on the carpet, I could see white residue up his nose. I was sick and said, "I can't pray for him. You can, but I can't". In the days that followed, when he was supposed to be at school events or at church, he wouldn't show up. From one day to the next, we didn't know if he was even going to come home.

Every summer, our church held vacation bible school and I would always take part. I needed to stay out of the house and keep the kids away from John as much as possible, so I signed up to teach the youth. Some days we went to vacation bible school so we could have something to eat. Looking at things from the outside, you never really know what a person is going through and no one knew the pain we were living through.

After going around and around the mulberry bush, time passed and things looked up and there was light at the end of the tunnel. John was establishing a relationship with our church and our pastors. Our pastors were also the godparents of our third child. John was a deacon in training and we saw some progress. One Sunday, Pastor Tony called John and two other men to the altar and spoke into their lives. He prophesied (said a specific thing would happen in the future) to my husband he would own his business painting automobiles. I jumped for joy and shouted all down the aisle of the church. A breakthrough was on the way and I was hoping this prophetic word would be the hope he needed to stay clean, to know there was a future, and to know God loved him so much even in the state he was currently in. That blew my mind. This is the reason Jesus died for us all who have sinned. The bible tells us, "for we all have sinned and fall short of the Glory of God." (Romans 3:23 NIV)

Since my profession was to help businesses start up, I knew the process and what it would take for us to open the business. To begin the process, we had to find information regarding everything needed from permits to business licenses. I knew very little about the auto body industry, but John knew the business inside and out since he had been working in that industry for over 14 years. I did my research and we created a step-by-step business plan. We had to think about marketing the business, who would take over if anything happened to him, insurance, employees, equipment, firewalls, air quality permits, occupancy permits, you name it, we had to learn about it. Once we were through that process, which took about six months, it was time to look for equipment and space.

Everything was falling into place. We found the perfect space for the shop at an affordable lease rate and proceeded to the next step of taking the business plan to the bank for equipment purchase and working capital for six months. I took our business plan to a few banks and the president of a local bank came through. He knew what we needed and what we did not need and was one of the best bank presidents we had the pleasure of working with. The most challenging part of the business was indeed the start-up process, and Mr. Carter took the risk with a start-up business and provided the much-needed financing for us. We hired an attorney to complete our incorporation paperwork and stock issuance, and we contacted an accountant to set the business up as an S-Corp with all of our accounting software and books. As soon as we had the capital needed to start, we began purchasing equipment and going through the necessary permitting and inspections process. Once our last inspections were completed and we had our occupancy permit, we were ready to open the doors for business!

We celebrated our grand opening with a local caterer grilling hamburgers, hot dogs, and chicken on-site. It was an amazing day with state and local officials, our pastors, friends, and family. Without the support of our pastor, we would not have been able to pull it off. He is such a humble and supportive man, and we could never repay him for all he did for us. Because of his support, we asked him to serve as our spiritual advisor and brought him in as a silent partner with stock ownership. I was elated and so proud of the man my husband was becoming.

John and our two employees were in the shop every day, and I continued to work my full-time job. His mother helped some days by answering the phone, and we had contracts with local dealerships to perform their car repairs. The shop was operating smoothly, producing excellent work, and cars were being completed in a professional and timely manner. In our first month, we grossed a significant amount of money and were well on our way to a prosperous year. Winter season, which is typically a good season for a body shop, was upon us and because of the snow and ice, accidents were bound to happen.

I started going to the shop in the evenings after work and on weekends to meet with the accountant and we noticed withdrawals were being made from the bank account, but the receipts were not being kept. I knew it was not a payroll issue because payroll was being handled automatically by the payroll company we were using. Something was going on and I was going to find out what was up. My first thought was whether John was using again and, if this was the case, I needed to talk to someone who could get through to him. I called our pastor, shared what I thought was going on, and he offered to have a talk with John. John explained to him he needed extra money to buy last-minute items for the business. Okay, that's fine, but we need to keep receipts so the books can be accurate. John said he would be sure not to lose receipts, track money he may take out, and put the receipts in the "in" basket on my desk. He started doing this and things were good, everything was being accounted for and the business was growing. Since opening the business, I was still working full-time, taking care of the kids and serving in the ministry. I continued to keep God at the forefront of my life and in the midst of everything going on I was completing ministerial classes to become an ordained minister.

Suddenly, I began to get calls at work about the shop opening late and on some days it was not opening at all. Cars were being messed up, mistakes were being made and some customers, who were also our friends, had to bring their car back several times before he got it right. Some sketchy characters were coming by the shop and our home and John would even bring some of them to church. One guy in particular just didn't sit well with my spirit, and I wondered why he was in our house and needed to spend the night. He stayed one night and after that I told John he had to go. This was going to stop before it went any further!

John played mind games with me so I had to stay 10 steps ahead of him. If I found drugs in the house, they weren't his, they belonged to someone who was there at the house with him. If he said he was working late at the shop, I would ride by there and no work was being done. He wasn't working, he wasn't even there. Excuses! He had an excuse for everything. I would ride through the streets looking for him in an attempt to save him from himself and truth be told, he didn't want to be saved and I honestly think he wanted to die. I tried to help him as much as I could and would go to the shop as often as I could to handle the customer service side of the business. Doing this and working a full-time job was difficult. We both knew we needed a full-time employee to handle the phones and customers, but we could not find anyone. It became overwhelming for John who was trying to do everything and just as fast as the business growth had happened, it began going downhill and spiraled out of control. I honestly believe John felt he didn't deserve the business or the success of the business and allowed it to fail on purpose. There needed to be more oversight during the day, not only for John, but with the other employees as well. One employee thought it was okay to go to the office desk, take out a check, order and pay for lunch with our business check and then put the receipt in my in box. Needless to say, he was let go. What I realized during this time was I did not want to own a business with my husband. You can only control yourself, you cannot control the actions of others, business partner or spouse.

I continued to serve as vice president of the company and became more involved with the paperwork and the finances of the office. John and I had several arguments about finances and how he should run the business, and bit by bit he started needing more and more money again. I was not willing to increase his pay, so he started writing his own checks.

As our financial troubles became worse, John's mother, a loving and kind person who has always been there for us no matter what, was still in denial about our situation and began giving him money. I tried to show tough love, but things worsened when she became his enabler. I understand no mother wants to admit their only son is an addict, even though deep down inside the truth is known. Talking to her about this situation was not an option, and even though she knew the signs, she was ignoring them.

While I was still working full time and helping to run the business, I was also preparing for my ordination ceremony. My father was coming to town for the ceremony, so I was trying to mask everything else and focus on this happy occasion. I left work early that day to go home and prepare for the ceremony and when I arrived at the church, my family was there, my father was there, but my mother was not. The relationship with my mother was being healed, but that is a story for another day. As the pastor began the ceremony for the seven of us who were being ordained that evening, it was a wonderful feeling of excitement, knowing to whom much is given, much is required. We all laughed, went to dinner and talked together. It felt normal.

The next day, I received a call from the landlord's wife reaching out to tell me rent payments were behind. Lord, what else is going to happen? In my eyes, this blessing has now turned into a curse. My pastor and I had an intervention with John at the shop. As if I thought it could not get any worse, we tried talking to him and he became more agitated and argumentative. The last thing I remember about the intervention was the two of us standing up in the office and having words back and forth. Now, I am about

5'2" on a good day and my husband is about 6'2" but I was fed up and had enough. I told him, "the Lord blessed you with a business many people would love to have and you are running it straight into the ground!" He acted like he was going to hit me and my pastor jumped in between us. Finally I said, "I wish you would hit me! I will have you arrested — go ahead, go ahead!" I turned my cheek so he could hit me. I was at my boiling point that day and tired of dealing with that demon. I was not having it. He turned and walked out of the shop as my pastor stood there trembling in disbelief at what had just happened. I looked at my pastor and said, "I told you he was using again. This is exactly how he has been acting lately. There is no talking to him and every conversation ends in an argument." My pastor responded, "we have to get him some help" and I'm here to tell you help couldn't come soon enough. John's mother gave him money to put into the business and of course some to put into his pocket. We could partially pay the rent but not get caught up. I was taking money from my paycheck to pay household bills and to keep the business running, and it became too much.

I had a heart to heart with my husband and told him he had a sickness and needed to get help soon. He had lost weight, looked sick, and when he agreed to go into an inpatient facility, I immediately began making calls to local facilities. I explained to them what my experience was in dealing with him— the agitation, the argumentative reactions and the happy and sad moments and when the intake person asked him if he was suicidal, and he responded "yes." That's when I realized he was truly hurting inside and felt there was no way out. He was caught in a cycle and couldn't get out.

Getting John into a treatment facility was a priority, and after several calls to different facilities, we finally received a call from an inpatient facility available to take him. The hoops we had to jump through with the insurance company created a lot of stress and no family should have to endure the emotional toll of trying to get a loved one help and treatment.

We shared the news with our pastor and my husbands' mother and John began packing for his 21-day rehab journey. The more we talked to him about getting clean, the more I could see he was trying to figure out a way to get out of going. If I had it my way, he was going no matter what. Here's my issue with not communicating your feelings to your spouse; if you are scared, say you are scared, if you are having second thoughts, say so. Stop holding your feelings inside and open your mouth to say what is wrong. I am not a mind reader. Effectively communicating your feelings to your spouse or anyone is the way to improve and build healthy relationships.

Packed and ready, we drive about an hour to the rehabilitation center. We get there and they need a $300 co-pay. It would have been nice if someone had mentioned while we were planning for John to be admitted a $300 co-pay would be required. This is where I have a real problem with the healthcare system. We have insurance, don't have a lot of money, and have to pay this money here and now or he could not be admitted. There is something wrong with this picture, but thankfully I had the money and wrote the check for his admission.

John was all checked in. We said our goodbyes, and I returned home. While John was in rehab, the landlord filed an eviction notice. I reached out to all the creditors of the business, planned to pay off the debts, and closed the doors to the business. The corporation was dissolved and that was the end of that. I was paying business and household bills but had a made-up mind it was time to make some personal moves for me and the children.

After getting the business debt paid off and selling the office furniture and equipment, I started saving money to purchase a home. It was time to move out of my mother-in-law's house and have our own home. John could stay with his mother or get his life together and come with us, but one thing I knew for sure, a change was going to come! The questions in my mind were, is this going to be his breaking point? Was this his rock bottom?

I could not visit him during the first week of rehab, but after the first week they wanted to hold family sessions with the spouse. During these sessions they explained how the first year of recovery was usually the most challenging, and discussed drug addiction statistics, such as the relapse rates for addiction being between 40-60%.

To an addict, the drug becomes a pleasure and although I just wish he would just stop using, it just wasn't a simple task. It sounds easy to me and others who have a loved one addicted to drugs, but it's harder than we could ever imagine. It stood out when the counselor said drug addiction is 100% preventable if you never use it. I listened more intently when he said that. What exactly did that mean? Well, what it meant was drug addiction is 100% preventable if you never pick it up. Sounds easy, doesn't it?

How many of you have tried drugs and never became addicted? How many of you have tried drugs and have become addicted? Genetics can play a role in addiction, which is why I have been quite honest with my children by telling them their grandfathers on both sides of the family were alcoholics. Educating people and talking about addiction is the best way to prevent addiction, which is why I wanted to share that early on with my children.

The counseling session really helped me and when it was time to share thoughts within the group, me and my gung-ho, full of faith, Christian self said "Well I'm believing God and having faith to believe my husband will not be in the relapse numbers and will stay clean when he gets out". Thinking about it now, I'm sure those folks were like "yeah, right lady. You are delusional." I didn't care what they thought, I believed what I said and that's all that mattered. It may sound crazy to those on the outside, but that is faith. I knew what God showed me — my husband clean and free from addiction and I was going to continue to trust God and believe.

The addiction was wearing on me and I was falling out of love with my husband. When he was high and using, I was too disgusted to even be close to him. I felt he was unclean and I could barely look at him, but while he was in rehab, the house was peaceful and I was happy. It wasn't just me, the children were also their best selves. The more I thought about how I wanted the pain to stop and how I was being consumed by the addiction, the less I cared about my marriage. I was taking his addiction out on my family and was being short with people because of how I felt and what I was dealing with. I didn't like that and had to learn how to be at peace even in the storm. I wanted to be the same person each day and not let his addiction disturb my peace or the peace of our children.

After weeks of rehab John was released and as anyone who has experienced this with a family member understands, he didn't seem like himself. His body had detoxed from not using for 21 days and he seemed sad. On the drive home, even though we talked very little, he talked about how hard the first week of going through detox was.

My husband had no idea about the man he had become. He was still wearing a mask, and it was going to take more to remove this mask. He had been wearing it for so long, it had become part of him, it had become who he was. He didn't realize we all looked at him differently because of his mood swings. He didn't know who the person was in the mirror, and I didn't know who the man was in the bed next to me each night. I just kept praying every day and speaking to God about seeing my husband clean in his future state and not his present state. I prayed his mind would be renewed and the taste of drugs would be removed from him.

Once John was out of rehab, he found a part-time job. I thought he would go back into the automotive repair field, but he went in a completely different direction. He began attending drug support group meetings held at the rehab center, and although we could tell he was struggling, he was honestly trying to do better.

When John was undergoing treatment, we were advised to take one day at a time and that was what we were doing. It felt like we were walking on eggshells, trying not to trigger his desire to use again. I kept as busy as possible because if I didn't, I would start thinking about my life and what our family was going through and that would lead me to feelings of depression. The kids and church became my life, and I began saving money and planning annual vacations for us to get away and do family things together.

We wanted to take the kids to Florida, so we planned a road trip. We packed up the jeep and left early one morning with a plan to reach Florida by midnight. John started out driving and was very talkative during the entire drive. We enjoyed a delightful conversation and when he got tired, I drove while he and the kids slept. Suddenly, the recap of a tractor-trailer tire flew off and hit a truck in the middle of the road. I was terrified and started turning the steering wheel from side to side. The jeep was swerving as I tried to avoid the tire recap and avoid an accident. All I could hear was John saying "hold it, hold it!" I swerved to avoid hitting another car, but still managed to hold it steady. Just like that, in the middle of the night, we were saved from having an accident and the driver of the tractor-trailer didn't even know what he had caused.

My heart was beating so fast. The kids never woke up and had no idea what had happened. All I could say was, "Thank you, Jesus! Thank you for your protection and for keeping us from harm and danger." About two hours later, around 1 a.m., we reached our hotel, checked in and got in a good night's sleep. The next morning, we headed to the pool for the day. It was nice to see the kids making friends with other vacationing kids, and it was good to see John in a good mood. I knew his body was in pain, but we had a wonderful time sightseeing and visiting Universal Studios. The week went by quickly and when it was time to pack and get on the road to head home, I wondered to myself, "why can't all of our weeks be like this one?" When we returned home, we were ready for a fresh start. John went back to his job, we were good, laughing and joking together, he was staying closer to home and we were on the mend. One night he wanted to go out with his old friend Antonio. I did not like Antonio and John knew it. I blamed Antonio for John's addiction because John told me Antonio was the one who introduced him to sniffing heroin. Keep in mind, drug addicts are the best liars in the game. He and Antonio went on their way and when they came back, I was pulling up to the house at the same time. John walked up the driveway and went into the house. Antonio put his car window down and said to me, "John has something to tell you." I said, "okay and how do you know that?" Antonio said, "He called me to talk and that's why we got together." I said, "alright, I will talk to him. What does he have to tell me?" He mumbled, "He doesn't know how to tell you he has relapsed." My response was "oh, really? Well, I guess we are going to have to have a conversation." After all the time and energy everyone put in to help John get into rehab and here we go, a relapse within 30 days of being home. Something is wrong and it goes deeper than the addiction.

I cannot tell you how the conversation went and I know you are tired of hearing me say this, but I was just tired. I was tired of going through, tired of trying to help, tired of being supportive—I was just tired. Again I sought spiritual advice and our pastors counseled us. This sounds like a good idea, right? Well, not so much. Our pastors were also family. We knew them and they knew us and I later realized this may not be the best mix to spiritual counseling, but at least we gave it a try. The first session was okay, but each session after that seemed to get worse instead of better. Our marriage seemed to be spiraling out of control. We were arguing at home and it seemed as if the enemy just kept beating us up. I didn't like my husband and he didn't like me. How were we ever going to live the married life God intended for us to live?

While dealing with my husband's addiction, which seemed to consume my life, I lost two people I loved very much — both of my grandmothers. One grandmother raised me and the other was supportive of me no matter what. My grandmother Cecelia would come over and help with the kids while I worked, which kept me from worrying about whether something would happen to them. Mama Cee Cee, as I called her, was my rock. I didn't have time to truly grieve because of everything else happening in my life. This addiction could no longer be my focus. My husband had to choose to live and not die, and my focus had to shift.

I co-chaired our women's retreat committee, along with our co-pastor. The women's retreat was an event we held annually. I was getting involved in church events and activities as much as I could. I began meditating and entrenching myself in the Word in the morning, during the day, and at night. On my job, I was promoted to a director's position which had me traveling around the world and I also began attending college, taking classes here and there.

Pastor Bethea was our speaker for the night and I remember sitting there feeling broken when she called me up to the front and said, "You have the gift of faith. No matter what you go through, know your faith will bring you through." At the next retreat, the speaker said to me, "You were created for greatness. There is something great for you in government and prosperity is upon you." I was getting stronger and was building my strength in this addiction cycle. I was one of the luncheon speakers and spoke from the book of Esther. My message was entitled "You Were Called For Such a Time As This." During my message, I shared some details of what I was going through and during it all, how I never thought I would feel as much pain as I did having a husband addicted to drugs. I shared with those ladies about the many nights I drove through the streets looking for my husband's vehicle to find him because he had not come home. As I was preaching to them, I was encouraging myself, and as I said to those ladies, "You were called for such a time as this," I could feel the breakthrough taking place in my life. God whispered, "Daughter, you were called for such a time as this! Breakthrough is now."

After speaking, the ladies let me know they had no idea I was going through what I was and they saw me as one who always kept her head up and encouraged everyone else. I am reminded of this quote from Real Talk Kim, "Somebody is watching you learning how to trust God and your example matters." I thank God I never looked beat up or down-trodden during this valley experience, and God shielded me while the enemy tried to break me and my family.

After many retreats, much studying, and self–examination, God showed me I did not need to pray for Him to fix my husband. Instead, I needed to pray for myself and understand there were some things God was trying to get out of me in order for me to bear much fruit. He showed me I needed to stop focusing on John and focus on myself.

I started praying daily for God to forgive me of any sins and to create in me a clean heart and renew a right spirit within me. (Psalm 51) I focused on God and deepening my relationship with Jesus. I had to remember God called me to minister the gospel, which meant leading others to Christ, applying the Word, and being an example. I asked God to raise me up to be a better wife, mother, friend, employee, and minister and to make me better and not bitter. No matter what comes from this point forward, I have the tools to overcome.

The more I shifted my focus, the more my husband started using and hanging out with people like him. One evening, we were supposed to attend a church dinner party at a fancy golf resort, so the kids and I were already there dressed up in our nice pretty clothes sitting at the table waiting for John to arrive. We mingled with the other members and played games. It was time to have dinner and no John. I started getting a funny feeling in my stomach, like something was wrong. You know those knots you sometimes get in your stomach when you feel something is wrong? Yep, those knots. I called his phone, no answer, called again, no answer. I decided I would not mention it to anyone, and I acted as if nothing was wrong.

John never arrived at the dinner party and I received a phone call later informing me he had taken his mother's car out of town to get a tire, and somehow he ended up with a group of addicts and allof them were being held at the city's jail. All of the individuals who had been with John were released on bail, and one of them came by the house to ask me if I was going to bail John out. My response was, "Absolutely not! He can stay there as long as he has to." Years ago I vowed I would not be putting up bail money for anybody unless it was a circumstance beyond control and this was not.

His mother's car had been impounded and she had no idea he had even taken her car out of town. After we made some calls, she was able to get her car back.

While John was locked up, I called my doctor and told him I wanted to have my tubes tied right away. If John and I were to get back together, I was not taking any chances of getting pregnant. The doctor scheduled the tubal; I had it done, and I was in and out with same-day surgery. After about 2 ½ weeks of John being in jail, I went to see an attorney about a separation. I told her where he was and I wanted full custody with supervised visitation and drug testing. I did not want to wait any longer and asked her to please serve him while he was in jail. The future looked bleak, and those who loved him were starting to give up. My heart went out to him, but I could not have this affecting my future or the future of our children. I didn't hear from John again until he had been in jail for 20 days. What kind of husband and father doesn't even bother to call his family to tell them he is in jail? This was it, and surely the Lord wanted me to separate from this chaos.

When John's hearing was scheduled, I decided not to visit or attend because I thought it was time for him to sit and think about what he wanted his future to look like. We had no contact with each other and the day before his hearing our pastor prayed a simple prayer, that God's will be done. I could tell, even he, as a pastor, was frustrated and disappointed.

The day after the hearing I learned John and the others who were arrested would not be charged and after serving 27 days in jail, John would be released. I'm not sure how he got home from jail, but three days after being released he showed up at the house and I did not recognize him. His hair had grown and he had not shaven in 27 days. He looked like a homeless person. Since we were living at his mother's house, I couldn't put him out, so my only option was to find my own place and move out. He showered and shaved and then wanted to sit down and talk to us. Will it devastate the children if we separate? When the kids arrived home, our youngest son ran to him, jumped up in his arms, wrapped his arms and legs around him, and said, "Daddy, don't leave me again!" I was in tears, but realized he was too young to know what was going on.

John's time in jail was longer than his time in rehab, so he got clean again while in jail. He told me while in jail, he was studying the Word. We hear that all the time from people who get locked up. He talked about leading prayer and helping others and he came out of jail on fire for God. He realized his life, as he knew it, could have been over and he shared with me how he cried out to the Lord and asked for a second chance to get his life together. God certainly granted him that chance.

On his first Sunday back to church, as the praise & worship team sang, he started jumping up and down and looked like he was breaking chains off of him. He was breaking free, he was clean.

John started looking for a job again and found a job at a local restaurant. Since he liked to cook, he thought he would enjoy something different as he got back on his feet. He enjoyed the job and was working on his road to recovery. Our church was affiliated with a larger church and it was helping him see a better life and connect with men who were prosperous and loved God. Little did we know this larger church would play a huge part in our future. John started attending church fellowship events for men and trying to do better. He was talking more, sharing his struggles, fighting the temptations coming his way and trying to fight the triggers. He fought a good fight, but the temptation kept knocking at the door. One day he could not fight any longer and he relapsed. He continued to work as he started the process all over again, trying to stay clean.

On a hot summer August day, the oldest kids were at home and our youngest was at daycare when I received a call from my mother-in-law at the office saying "The house is on fire." At first I thought she was kidding or playing a joke on me, but when I realized she was telling the truth I hung up and ran past my employees saying "our house is on fire." One of my employees ran after me and volunteered to drive me because I was in no shape to drive. When we arrived at the house, the fire department, our neighbors and our pastor were all standing outside. I knew the fire chief and tearfully asked him about our pet cat. Sadly to say, we lost our rescue cat, Mac. The kids were devastated and John was nowhere to be found or reached.

This was not the time to break, this was the time to gird my loins, fight the good fight of faith and fight the enemy with the

Word. This was a fixed fight and I was determined to win! I will see the goodness of the Lord in the land of the living. This too shall pass. The warning comes before destruction and this was yet another warning!

Sometimes, you just have to encourage yourself and that is what I did. I was more determined than ever to be free. We received so much love and outpouring of support after the fire. Later, I found out our oldest son had walked out of the house to go down the street, and moments after he left the house, the sound of an explosion was heard. It was reported flames could be seen from the highway, and when I heard this, I was thankful. I was thankful none of my children were in the house or died in a fire that day. My emotions were high and the thought of losing my kids made me sick to my stomach. God's protection has been around us and has kept us all from hurt, harm, and danger.

A window air conditioner unit sent an electrical surge through the house which caused the fire. I walked into the house and saw nothing left but the wooden part of the blue rocking chair I sat in to rock our son to sleep. We lost everything except the clothes we had on our backs when we left the house that morning. With the exception of our kitty, every material thing could be replaced. The Red Cross and the insurance company came immediately to the scene to bring checks, and the community support was overwhelming. One of my co-workers started a relief fund for us, and my cousin Nikki came by and gave us cash. Checks were coming in every day, churches were helping and the love shown was truly amazing. People were making us dinner so we didn't have to cook and we were able to get enough clothes for all five of us. After about a week I returned to work and we ended up staying with my mother-in-law in a neighbor's vacant house.

Here comes another stressor to add to my life. My family and my mother-in-law together for the next seven or more months was going to be a test for me, and I wasn't sure I was going to pass. Now, don't get me wrong I love my mother-in-law, but I would not want to stay with my mother for seven months. It makes you feel as if you are a child again.

While staying with my mother-in-law, we hit some bumps. John still had addiction issues, but they were manageable until he started acting a fool towards our oldest son. I was not sure what the issue was, but he would just pick on him for no reason. One Sunday morning before church they got into a fight in the house. John had crossed the line by putting his hands on our son and I promised our son it would not happen again — and it never did. One day we would have our own home and would not have to deal with that anymore.

Chapter VI
Restoration & Refreshing

John was falling back into his old ways and tricks of lying and whatever else he could do to satisfy his cravings and withdrawal symptoms. For the first time, things began going missing in the house. I lost jewelry and I believe he took it.

While the house was being rebuilt, I used those seven months as an opportunity to make plans for me and my children's future. Little by little, I tucked money away. I had money automatically deposited from my paycheck into my savings account, and I reached out to a friend in the mortgage business to discuss how I could get a mortgage. She told me about the different programs and exactly what I needed to do. While the contractors were rebuilding the house which was destroyed by fire, I was building savings and planning a way out.

After seven months, the house was ready and even as we moved back in, I knew the kids and I would not be there long. I never shared my plan with anyone, just started making moves in silence. All things were new and we were back in the house. Since the home was my mother-in-law's, the insurance money for the fire went to her to replace the furniture and the lost items. We picked out new furniture and almost everything that was destroyed was replaced. The house had been rebuilt from the inside out.

John still did not have a job, so what does his mother do? She gave him thousands of dollars to purchase a vehicle to make up for the items he lost in the fire. What was the logic behind giving a drug addict thousands of dollars to go buy a vehicle? We both knew all the money was not used to purchase a vehicle, and if I were a gambling person, I would bet money on it. I was infuriated beyond measure and knew I definitely had to move forward with my plans to purchase a home with or without my husband.

At first, John was not in agreement with purchasing a home and moving. Shortly after we moved back to the rebuilt home, my mother-in-law told us she was moving back into the house. She was living in her fiancés' house who passed away. His daughter was moving back to live in the house. After learning this, we both knew we needed our own independence so we could start over. I was approved for a mortgage loan and began house hunting until we finally found the perfect house. It was out of my price range and the builder said he could not reduce the price of the model home we initially wanted, but he offered to build us a new home on another lot within our price range and throw in some kitchen upgrades. All I could do was say, "Thank you, Lord!" The builder and I began working together and I shared with John some things I was doing. He did not seem to be excited, and I believe fear was sneaking in. He would rather stay in his mother's house forever, and if he decided to do that, the choice would be his. I am sure many feelings were going on inside of him, and I can imagine perhaps he was feeling less than a man or feeling down because he could not provide for his family.

Things with the new house moved rather quickly, and lot #8 was the lot we chose. The number eight represents a new beginning. I worked with an amazing realtor who was also a friend, and the only other thing needed were closing costs. I consulted with the builder on colors and appliances, and brick by brick I watched them construct our home. John and I started communicating better and I told him if he decided to move with us to the new home, the drugs could not be a part of it. He acknowledged my ultimatum and knew he had to get help and stick with it. He found a full-time job and nine months later, we were packed and ready to move into our brand-new home. John said he was committed to making things work and getting clean, the kids were happy and everyone was willing to commit to a new start.

One day as I was doing laundry, I found a bag which previously had drugs in it. My first thought was "John must have had it in his pants pocket and left it there". I brushed it off and meanwhile, I continued to pray. I threw it in the trash and didn't say a word to him about it. Then one day we were having a conversation and I said to him, "I want to remind you, whatever is done in the dark will always manifest in the light. For nothing is secret that will not be revealed, nor anything hidden that will not be known and come to light." (Luke 8:17)

After being in the new home for exactly one month, the Lord woke me up around 1 a.m. I'm not sure what it is with 1 a.m. but the Holy Spirit instructed me to go into the bathroom. I noticed something on the floor, but I kept going. On my way to the sink, I noticed it again. After washing my hands, I bent down to pick up whatever it was and it was a tiny bag with brown residue in it. I couldn't tell by looking at it, but whatever was in it was gone. I smelled it and recognized that scent. It was heroin residue which had the scent of a vitamin. I became very familiar with that scent so anytime John used it, I could smell it when he came close to me. I started picking up on things to look for so I would know if he was using. When I found the bag this time, I felt different than before; this time I was at peace.

I took the baggie to John and asked him straight up, "What was this?" He told me it was brown sugar. I just looked at him like, "You think I am stupid, don't you? Do I look slow to you? All these years and you don't think I got hip to your game? I'm wiser than I was before." He stepped outside and when he came back in he reluctantly admitted he was using again. I demanded he leave the house until he had himself together. He had once again chosen drugs over his family. He confessed how relieved he was since now the hiding was over. He packed his clothes and left the house. When I compare that moment with similar moments of the past, I noticed there was a difference. This time, I had taken control of my life and the lives of our children. This time, I had my head on straight. I had worked hard and lived through hell to get us to a place of home ownership and sacrificed a lot to save money to buy the house. I did it with no help from him, and I would be darned if I was going to subject my kids to this behavior again.

I was hoping John would learn a lesson by being asked to leave, but his mother allowed him to stay with her. Once again he was jobless but had food, a roof over his head, and money in his pocket. His mother was enabling him yet again. Reality could not set in because whenever he would fall, she would be there to catch him instead of allowing him to handle his problems like a grown man with a wife and family. This was a sore spot for me, but just like everything else, I sought the Lord for guidance to lead, guide and direct my mother-in-law in making decisions as it related to her son.

John and I remained separated until we began seeing a licensed marriage counselor and a therapist to help him with his addiction. Sitting with this counselor was exactly what we needed at this very point in our lives. He was a pastor, but also a licensed counselor and therapist, which truly made a difference in our lives. This time felt different and both John and I had reached the point where we were both willing to call it quits and divorce if this counseling did not work.

We learned how to communicate with each other and things we had not admitted to each other were admitted during our sessions. We learned about the five love languages, which was something neither of us knew about. We were both young going into this marriage and there was so much we did not know. We realized together, we made plenty of mistakes and when we had our first child, we didn't know how to be parents. We were learning as the years passed, but you can only do better when you know how to do better. The sessions exposed us to things we did not even know were problems within our marriage. Trust was a major part of my concern, and Dr. Ball taught us how to work through it. The sessions revealed my lack of respect for my husband. Little by little the respect came and so did improvements. Dr. Ball opened our eyes to so many things which saved our marriage.

After our counseling sessions were over, we reconciled and starting working day by day not only on ourselves but on our marriage. After counseling, John said, "watch things get better; each year things are going to be better." I was leary and watched closely as he went through his daily routine of working and coming home. He was determined to not only say he was going to do better, but to reflect that with his actions as he helped around the house with the cleaning and cooking. We started traveling to actively take part in Marriage Made EZ for married couples with

Drs. Mike and Dee Dee Freeman. Brick by brick, precept by precept, we were rebuilding our marriage. He was showing honor and respect to me and I was doing the same. We were working together to accomplish family goals.

When Christmas approached, John asked me to get a Christmas list from the kids. He wanted to do all the shopping and all I had to do was wrap the gifts. This was truly a blessing. In the past, we would go half on everything and now that he had a full-time job and was clean, things were quite different. He was taking on household chores such as cleaning and cooking, giving me a break when I was tired, stressed, or taking classes. It was a new day and finally no more walking in darkness. My husband was finally becoming the man I knew he could be. He was saving money for our future and making plans to start a business.

One night I got sick–sicker than I'd ever been before. I had a fever for days and the doctor gave me antibiotics and said the fever was going to break in a few days. Well, the fever went down, but it did not go away. I remember John being in the bed with me trying to make me as comfortable as possible and all I could do was cry and lay my head in his lap. He rubbed my head and comforted me saying "Honey, anything you need me to do I will do it. What can I do to make you feel better?" The only thing I asked for was a cup of hot herbal tea with lemon and honey. He would check on me practically every hour through the night to make sure I was okay. That was the sweet, caring husband I knew. I was sick for almost a week and he was right there to help me and take care of the house while working.

I attribute the turnaround in our marriage to our former pastors and to our current pastor and his wife. The two of them are so authentic and transparent, which helped us tremendously. We started having date nights, family meetings and used the information we were receiving at church to improve our lives. We now look at each other with love in our hearts, no longer tolerating each other but truly loving one another. The wedding vows are real and are a covenant we certainly felt like breaking; however, through sickness and in health, we survived. We have a healthy, God-centered marriage. That addiction came to break us as individuals, break us as a family, break our children and ultimately destroy us. We stood and fought, we bent but we never broke. We were taken through the fire and came out as pure gold, and we were pressed like olives and came out with fresh oil. We were renewed through this situation.

We are where we are today because of the many people who poured into our lives during that tough time. We can stand today and say by the grace of God we made it. He is finally free from drug addiction. He takes one day at a time and continues to gain wisdom and understanding to be the best husband, father, and man of God. The mask has been removed! Will you be so courageous and remove your mask?

Words from the Husband

One day while driving down the road in my car, from out of nowhere, the Lord showed me a fence in a vision. One side of the fence was nice and beautiful with green grass, bright yellow, and vibrant colored flowers. It was sunny with families and people laughing and enjoying themselves.

On the other side of the fence there was dirt, no grass, darkness, cloudiness, gray skies, a stormy look in the sky, and a bunch of sick people slumped over and walking slowly. They attempted to cross over to the other side where it was sunny and bright, but they could not cross over. I could see both sides and could cross from the desolated dark side to the sunny side, which was full of life.

At that point, I realized I had a problem, I pulled over to the shoulder of the road and cried. That was the beginning of me being able to come out of darkness into the light. I was shown I had a chance to get to the other side and God had given me a choice. I could either stay in the dark state I was in or move to the light and be among the land of the living. At that very moment, I chose life and knew this would not be an overnight process. It took me trying over and over and over to be free. It was a long process, but I was determined I was not giving up. I got up and fell, got up and fell. Going to rehab helped, but did not solve my problems. It takes patience and believing you can be free from this addiction, but you cannot do it alone.

When I realized I was so deep in my addiction, I asked myself, "What have you done to yourself?" I remembered when I was young, my grandmother prayed for me and told me I was going to do great things. I wanted to be that person again. I suffered daily, detoxed cold turkey and it was misery with the pain being unbearable. Patience came first and I had to take it one day at a time as they told me in rehab. I never knew what that meant until I was ready to get clean. I encourage anyone suffering from addiction to take it one day at a time and don't focus on a week, a month, or a year — start at day one.

I stayed home and did not go out. I separated myself from the people I used to get high with because it was a trigger. You must control who you are around, especially the ones you got high with in order to get clean and stay clean. I had to change people, places, and things. I surrounded myself with loved ones, and through the painful withdrawal symptoms, I kept moving. I read the bible and could not understand it until I got another version. I prayed and read the Word to help me get through. Finally, I was at a place where back steps were less and less and then they were gone completely and I was free.

Even if your mind is telling you to go out and have fun (meaning to get high) don't! This is what I did:

1. Be Patient.

2. Be Still and seek God.

3. Surround yourself with loved ones or people who will motivate you and not ones who will look down on you, judge you and criticize you. Get around people who will speak life over you.

4. Exercise.

5. Have an accountability partner.

Every person's walk is not the same. Some may need rehab, a transition home, meetings, etc., but the key thing is to do what takes you to the path of being free and clean. If you don't have a church, seek one and they may have a group which helps those suffering or who have suffered from addiction. Having a positive pastor who leads by example was important then and still is and it also helped save my life. Everyone needs a good pastor. Find one who complements who you are and then serve them. As you serve them, also allow them to escort you into your next level.

Words from the Eldest Son

From my perspective, and looking back, I feel the best thing that could have happened was for my father to leave or for my parents to declare me homeless so I would not have had to stay in that environment. Although I am good now, I would not want any child to grow up in a house where either parent is on drugs. It is too emotional for a child and I feel like I was messed up because of it.

EPILOGUE

NIH defines drug addiction as a chronic disease characterized by compulsive drug seeking and use despite harmful consequences and changes in the brain, which can be long lasting. These changes in the brain can lead to the harmful behaviors seen in people who use drugs. Drug addiction is also a relapsing disease. Relapse is the return to drug use after an attempt to stop.

Many families suffer from drug addiction and it is a nasty disease. This book was written to share the experiences I endured as a wife and how it affected our entire family. In our day-to-day living, we never know what a person is going through, and sometimes it's not for us to know. Allow the Holy Spirit to lead and guide you, and when he does, he will intentionally put individuals in your path to help you. It may be a hug you needed that day, a smile, or encouragement. Whatever it is, be open to hear from God.

While facing this challenge in my life, I was holding my head high and going through this affliction. I was accepting various awards, serving as president of local associations and receiving promotions. I want you to know the key is to go through and not get stuck. Don't stop to have a pity party and look like you are going through. Make sure God gets the glory even when you are going through. Your maturity and growth in Christ will be reflected when you go through. The way you handle a crisis in your life will determine how well you model being an example of Christ at that moment. In the valley and on the mountain top Christ is to be exalted.

During this time in my life, I had to decide to fight and I encourage those of you who are in this situation or a similar situation to fight. Fight for your family, fight for your children, fight for your marriage, FIGHT! Don't give up, hold on.

As I was going through this affliction, there were honestly sincere people who I could turn to for advice and prayer. Certainly, I sought God, always, but sometimes you want the comfort of talking to an actual person you can trust. You actually need someone you know you can freely share how you are feeling and what is going on and not hear it again. We all have felt the hurt of telling someone something in confidence, even within the church, and hearing it again. I found those trustworthy people and held them close. What the enemy meant for evil, God has turned it around for His good.

My husband was always a man with a heart to help others and he has helped many. He needed help to get out of his darkness and finally help came and he is now in God's marvelous light.

RESOURCES

1. Contact your local church to see if they have an addiction/recovery program.
2. Substance Abuse and Mental Health Services Administration, 1-800-662-4357
3. Reach out to your local health provider or mental health provider
4. Celebraterecovery.com

How to Help Your Loved One or Friend

1. Don't be an enabler. Family, friends, and parents do not enable the individual who is using. No matter how much you may feel sorry for them, do not give them money and do not feed their behavior by offering them a place to stay.

2. Do not force them to get help. As much as you want them to get help, they have to want it on their own. Forcing them means they are only doing it because you are forcing them to, not because they believe they have a problem and want help.

3. Don't belittle or be negative. Try words of encouragement and most importantly, listen.

4. Do your research and educate yourself. Learn about drug addiction and how it affects the brain specifically how the risk/reward center of the brain has been rewired with the cravings and drug use.

5. Understand, an addict cannot stop anytime they want. I had to learn this and the thing you have to be mindful of is once they become an addict, they lose control and it is no longer a choice for them. At this point, they need help to stop the addiction.

6. Do not take responsibility for the addict. Let the addict be responsible for their behavior, appearance, appointments, etc.

7. Do not put your feelings above the addicts. Be sure to take time for yourself and not put the feelings of the addict above you or your family.

8. Don't focus on "fixing" your loved one. Your loved one has to want to fix themselves.

9. Set personal boundaries. Make sure you set rules and expectations and if they are not followed, effectively communicate consequences.

10. Discuss underlying reasons or causes of the drug addiction.

11. Encourage them to get help and treatment.

12. As much as you may want to fight this fight for your loved one, you can't.

13. Get help from a therapist and/or a spiritual leader.

ABOUT THE AUTHOR

Keasha Haythe has been an Economic Development Professional for 19 years and served as Director for Dorchester County. She developed a track record of initiating sound policies and innovative strategies to foster economic growth. Partnering with private and public stakeholders, she championed education, entrepreneurship and expansion of existing businesses as key economic drivers.

Ms. Haythe is owner of Zoe Economic Development Group, LLC., an economic development consulting firm and is president and founder of the Foundation of HOPE, Inc., a non-profit organization.

Ms. Haythe holds a degree in Business Administration and is a Certified Economic Developer. She served on the Board of Directors for the Maryland Economic Development Association, and was appointed by Governor Larry Hogan to serve on the Maryland Marketing Partnership Board.

Ms. Haythe is an Ordained Minister and a member of Spirit of Faith Christian Center. She is married to Marcus L. Haythe Sr., and they have three children; Marcus Jr., Miniah and Isaiah.

www.ingramcontent.com/pod-product-compliance
Lightning Source LLC
LaVergne TN
LVHW010107110826
845155LV00028B/523

* 9 7 8 1 9 5 2 7 5 6 4 3 6 *